The Heinemann Illustrated Encyclopedia

Volume 10
Tou-Zim

First published in Great Britain by Heinemann Library
Halley Court, Jordan Hill, Oxford OX2 8EJ
a division of Reed Educational and Professional Publishing Ltd.

OXFORD MELBOURNE AUCKLAND
JOHANNESBURG BLANTYRE GABORONE
IBADAN PORTSMOUTH NH (USA) CHICAGO

Series Editors: Rebecca and Stephen Vickers
Author Team: Rob Alcraft, Catherine Chambers, Jim Drake,
Fred Martin, Angela Royston, Jane Shuter, Roger Thomas,
Rebecca Vickers, Stephen Vickers
Reading Consultant: Betty Root

Photo research by Katharine Smith
Designed and Typeset by Gecko Ltd
Printed in Hong Kong by Wing King Tong

02 01 00 99 98
10 9 8 7 6 5 4 3 2 1

ISBN 0 431 09061 0

British Library Cataloguing in Publication Data.

The Heinemann illustrated encyclopedia
1. Children's encyclopedias and dictionaries
I. Vickers, Rebecca II. Vickers, Stephen, 1951–
032

ISBN 0431090629

Acknowledgements:
Cover: The cover illustration is of a male specimen of *Ornithoptera goliath*, commonly called the
Goliath Birdwing. Special thanks to Dr George C. McGavin and the Hope Entomological
Collections, Oxford University Museum of Natural History.

J. Allan Cash Ltd: pp7b, 9, 10b, 11t, 13, 16, 18, 20, 21b, 22, 29, 33t, 46. **BBC Natural History Unit:**
Jeff and Sue Turner – p37b. **Bruce Coleman:** Atelier and Kohler – p47b. **Hulton Getty:** pp6t, 10t,
42, 43. **The Hutchison Library:** p48; John G. Egan – p17; Robert Francis – p24; Melanie Friend –
p45. **Natural History Museum:** p23t. **Oxford Scientific Films:** p30b; Kathie Atkinson – p44b;
G.I. Bernard – 47t; Neil Bromhall – p40b; Scott Camazine – p26; Daniel J. Cox – p38b; Jack
Dermid – p14t; Ken M. Johns – p41L; Richard Kolar – p35t; Lon E. Lauber – p11b; Tom Lauber –
p28t; Jeff Lapore – p37t; London Scientific Films – p40t; Tom McHugh – p38t; Richard Packwood –
p21t; M. Reardon – p14b; David Thompson – p28b; K.G. Vock – p30t. **Panos:** Jeremy Hartley – p19.
Science Photo Library: BSIP LECA – p4b; Gordon Garradd – p34; Soames Summerhays – p27t.
Stockphotos Inc.: Amanda Clement – p36t. **Thames Water Picture Library:** p31. **Tony Stone
Worldwide:** p12; Peter Dazeley – p23b; Paul Harris – p33b; Chris Kapolka – p5t; Martin Koretz –
p6b; Tom Tracey – p39b. **Werner Forman Archive:** p25.

Every effort has been made to contact copyright holders of any material
reproduced in this book. Any omissions will be rectified in subsequent printings
if notice is given to the Publisher.

Welcome to the
Heinemann Illustrated Encyclopedia

What is an encyclopedia?

An encyclopedia is an information book. It gives the most important facts about a lot of different subjects. This encyclopedia has been specially written for children your age. It covers many of the subjects from school and others you may find interesting.

What is in this encyclopedia?

In this encyclopedia each topic is called an entry. There is one page for every entry. The entries in this encyclopedia are on:

- animals
- plants
- dinosaurs
- countries
- geography
- history
- world religions
- music
- art
- transport
- science
- technology

How to use this encyclopedia

This encyclopedia has eleven books, called volumes. The first ten volumes contain entries. The entries are all in alphabetical order. This means that Volume One starts with entries that begin with the letter 'A' and Volume Ten ends with entries that begin with the letter 'Z'. Volume Eleven is the index volume and has some other interesting information in its Fact Finder section.

Here are two entries, showing you what you can find on a page:

The See also *line tells you where to find other related information.*

This is the letter that the entry starts with.

Fact boxes give you details about the topic.

Did You Know? *boxes have fun or interesting bits of information.*

The Fact File *tells you important facts and figures.*

Touch

See also: Smell, Taste

Touch is one of the senses. Touch is used by human beings and other animals to tell them about their surroundings. The skin is the part of the body that is sensitive to touch.

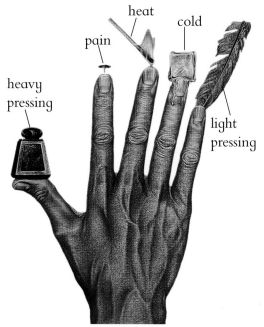

The five kinds of touch.

The five kinds of touch

The skin is sensitive to five kinds of touch: pain, heat, cold, heavy pressing and light pressing. Pathways in the body called nerves carry messages about touch to the brain. The fingertips and the lips have the most of the special sense cells that take the feelings of touch to the nerves.

Using touch

People who can't see clearly use their sense of touch more. They can learn to read using Braille. This uses patterns of raised dots that can be felt and read with the sensitive skin on the fingertips.

Animals that live in the dark can have a very good sense of touch. Fish, such as the catfish, that live in dark or muddy water have 'feelers' called barbels. These hang down under the fish's mouth so that it can feel what is below it.

Braille's tiny dots make letters which can be felt and read by blind people.

DID YOU KNOW?

Many animals have special long and sensitive hairs called whiskers. They use these to help them move about safely in the dark. Whiskers can tell them whether an opening is wide enough for them to go through.

Train

See also: Railway, Transport

A train is a powerful machine which runs on railway tracks. Trains take people or goods from one place to another.

The first trains

The first trains were built nearly 200 years ago. They had steam engines. In 1829 a train reached 47 kph. This was faster than anyone had ever gone before. Today trains are driven by diesel engines or electricity. They are very powerful, and can travel at over 260 kph.

People and trains

Trains are good at carrying lots of people and goods quickly and cheaply. Underground trains are used for transport in cities around the world.

TRAIN FACTS

FIRST TRAIN	1804, UK
FASTEST STEAM TRAIN	1938, 202 kph, UK
BIGGEST ENGINE	1940s, 534 tonnes, USA
FASTEST TRAIN	1990, 515 kph, France

French TGV trains can reach speeds of up to 515 kph. They hold the world speed record for trains.

The first passenger steam trains had open-sided carriages.

Transport

See also: Road

Transport is the way that people or goods are moved from place to place. Trains, cars and horse carts are all forms of transport.

The first transport

Thousands of years ago, people carried everything themselves. They were the transport. Then people trained donkeys and horses to carry things for them. They used boats to travel on water. When the wheel was invented, it was easier for people and animals to carry heavy loads.

Transport today

Today there are powerful engines for cars, trains, boats and aeroplanes. People can fly long distances in a few hours.

In many areas of the world where people cannot afford cars, transport has not changed much. People still walk and use animals to carry things.

Modern transport can travel fast, but too much traffic often holds them up.

TRANSPORT FIRSTS

FIRST BOATS	prehistoric times
FIRST WHEELED CARTS	3500 BC
FIRST HORSE-DRAWN BUS	1662
FIRST STEAM SHIPS	1802
FIRST STEAM TRAIN	1804
FIRST CARS	1885
FIRST AEROPLANES	1903

Some different forms of transport in London in the 1890s.

DID YOU KNOW?

Someone who travels on a form of transport is called a passenger. People who travel from home to work are called commuters.

Tree

See also: Forest, Rainforest, Wood

Trees are the largest plants. Broad-leafed trees have broad, flat leaves. In cold places, they lose their leaves in the autumn. Conifers have thin leaves, like needles. Most conifers are called evergreens because they have leaves all year round.

Bark to protect the living wood underneath

Leaves to take in light, carbon dioxide and water

An English oak

Trunk to hold the tree up and carry water and minerals to the leaves and branches

The life of a tree

Most trees grow from seeds which have fallen onto the ground. A young tree is called a seedling until it is about as high as an adult person. Then it is called a sapling. Many trees growing together are called a wood or a forest. Trees can grow in most places on land except where it is very cold, dry or windy.

People use trees in many ways. Some trees produce fruits or nuts. Other trees produce rubber, cork and wood gums. Wood from trees is used in buildings and to make furniture, toys and paper.

DID YOU KNOW?

The tallest trees in the world are the Giant Sequoias. They can grow to over 110 m tall.

This woman in Sri Lanka is a rubber tapper. She is collecting sap from the tree, to make rubber.

Triceratops

See also: Dinosaur, Fossil

The triceratops was a big, three-horned dinosaur. It had a heavy, bony head that was as long as a tall man. A triceratops weighed as much as a modern-day elephant.

TRICERATOPS FACTS

COLOUR........... not known
LENGTH........... 9 m
WEIGHT........... 5.5 tonnes
FIRST FOSSILS
FOUND............. 1880s, USA

Big, bony neck plate to protect the head from enemies' teeth. It also helped to keep triceratops cool

Horns on the head for fighting

Long, bony head

Tail for balance and fighting

Self-sharpening teeth

Triceratops

Lifestyle

The triceratops lived 65 million years ago. It was one of the last dinosaurs. There were many kinds of triceratops. They lived in groups or herds, eating low-growing plants. Their horns and giant heads were good for fighting off attackers such as tyrannosaurs.

FOOD

Triceratops ate low branches and leaves. They had self-sharpening teeth. As triceratops chewed, each tooth would wear down to a new, sharp edge.

Trinidad and Tobago

See also: South America

These islands are in the Caribbean Sea. Three lines of hills cross Trinidad. There are swamps in the east and west. Tobago is low land. There are mountains covered in forests in the east. Summers are hot. Winters are warm.

These workers are making beach umbrellas for tourists on Tobago.

Living and working

Over half the people in Trinidad and Tobago live in cities. There are mines and factories. Lots of oil is produced. Farmers grow sugar cane, cocoa, coffee, coconuts, citrus fruits and rice. Fishing is an important industry.

The population of Trinidad and Tobago is a mixture of people whose families were from Africa, Asia and South America.

DID YOU KNOW?

Trinidad is famous for its carnival in Port-of-Spain. There are fantastic costumes. People sing calypsos and play in steel bands, on oil-drum instruments.

People from other countries go to Trinidad and Tobago for holidays. They enjoy the spicy food, the beautiful beaches and the traditional calypso music.

SOUTH
AMERICA

FACT FILE

PEOPLE	Trinidadians, Tobagans
POPULATION	1.3 million
MAIN LANGUAGES	English, Spanish, Hindi, Creole
CAPITAL CITY	Port-of-Spain
MONEY	Trinidad and Tobago dollar
HIGHEST MOUNTAIN	Cerro Aripe – 940 m
LONGEST RIVER	River Ortoire – 50 km

Truck

See also: Road, Transport

A truck is a large, heavy vehicle used for carrying goods on roads. Trucks can have up to eighteen wheels. They have a place for the driver to sit at the front, called a cab. Trucks are also called lorries.

The first trucks

The first trucks were built a hundred years ago. They were powered by steam or electric engines. After the diesel engine was invented, most trucks were powered by diesel.

People and trucks

Trucks are useful because they can pull very heavy loads. Almost all of the things people buy and use have been carried by trucks. Trucks take large boxes or containers from factories, farms, ports and railways.

There are many trucks used for special purposes. Fire engines, refrigerated trucks, dustcarts and towing trucks are all special trucks.

TRUCK FACTS

FIRST TRUCKS....	1896, Germany
LONGEST...........	174 m, the Arctic Snow Train with 54 wheels, USA
WEIGHT...........	up to 40 tonnes

This 1921 delivery lorry has a petrol engine, but some deliveries then were still made with horse-drawn vans and carts.

Huge trucks, like this, are sometimes called juggernauts.

Tundra

See also: Arctic

Tundra is the name given to the very cold places along the Arctic Circle. There is tundra in the north of Asia, Europe and North America.

Tundra weather

The temperature is below freezing for most of the year in tundra areas. It can be as cold as −40°C in winter. A few months in the summer are just above freezing at 0°C. It is usually very dry in the tundra, though it does snow.

Life in the tundra

In winter, when the tundra is frozen over, some animals move south. Others hibernate and do not come out again until the summer. In summer, the top layers of soil thaw out and the ground becomes marshy. Then small plants such as mosses, lichens and short grasses grow. Herds of musk oxen, caribou and reindeer go to the tundra to graze. There are also smaller animals such as lemmings, rabbits, foxes and swarms of mosquitoes.

Not many people live in tundra areas. The Inuit of North America and the Lapps of Scandinavia have lived there for a long time.

This Lapp family lives in the tundra areas in the summer.

DID YOU KNOW?

High, flat areas in mountains can have a kind of tundra. This is called alpine tundra.

Some tundra areas turn green during the short summer.

Tunisia

See also: Africa

Tunisia is a country in north Africa. There are mountains in the north-west and hills in the south-east. There are lowlands with salt lakes. The coast has good farm land. It is hot and dry in the south. The north is wetter and warm.

Some people travel by camel in parts of Tunisia. Woven rugs with bright patterns cover the camels' backs.

Living and working

Many people in Tunisia live in cities along the coasts. There are mines and factories. Farmers grow fruit, dates and olives. Tunisians enjoy eating a semolina cake made with crushed dates and honey. There are herds of sheep, goats, cattle and camels.

Many tourists go to enjoy the sunny beaches and shop in the busy markets. Fine leatherwork and silk carpets are made in Tunisia.

DID YOU KNOW?

The capital city, Tunis, is built near the ruins of the ancient city of Carthage. It was the centre of a great empire about 2100 years ago.

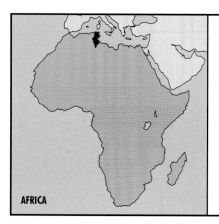

AFRICA

FACT FILE

PEOPLE........................ Tunisians
POPULATION .... 8.7 million
MAIN LANGUAGES .... Arabic, French
CAPITAL CITY.............. Tunis
MONEY....................... Tunisian dinar
HIGHEST MOUNTAIN.... Jeb el Chambi – 1544 m
LONGEST RIVER........... River Majardah – 360 km

Turkey

See also: Asia, Europe

Turkey is a country in the Middle East. The biggest part of Turkey is in Asia, but there is also a small part in Europe. The weather is mild and wet in winter, and it is hot and dry in summer. It snows in the mountains in the winter.

Living and working

Just under half the people in Turkey work on farms. Farmers raise sheep and grow figs and cotton. Cloth and goods such as rugs are made from the cotton in factories.

Tourists go to Turkey for the beaches, good weather and to see ancient ruins.

Lamb is often cooked over an open fire. Food is sometimes wrapped in vine leaves. People drink small cups of strong Turkish coffee.

The huge covered market in Istanbul sells everything from brassware to olives.

DID YOU KNOW?

The highest mountain in Turkey, Mount Ararat, is said to be the place where Noah's Ark came to rest after a great flood. This story is in the Bible.

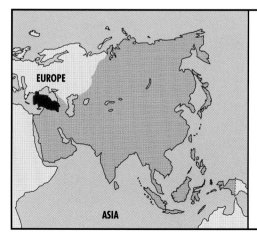

EUROPE

ASIA

FACT FILE

PEOPLE....................... Turks, Turkish

POPULATION .... 60.8 million

MAIN LANGUAGE......... Turkish

CAPITAL CITY..............Ankara

LARGEST CITY............ Istanbul

MONEY...................... Turkish lira

HIGHEST MOUNTAIN... Mount Ararat – 5165 m

LONGEST RIVER.......... Kizl Irmak – 1150 km

Turtle

See also: Reptile, Tortoise

A turtle is a reptile with a hard shell. It can swim in water. There are large turtles which live in the sea, and smaller turtles which live in rivers, lakes and ponds. Small turtles are sometimes called terrapins.

TURTLE FACTS

COLOUR	brown or green
LENGTH	up to 2 m
WEIGHT	up to 300 kg
STATUS	some endangered
LIFE SPAN	about 70 years
ENEMIES	birds, fish, crabs, people

Turtle families

A female sea turtle may swim for hundreds of kilometres to lay her eggs on the same beach where she was born.

Some female turtles lay 200 eggs. She digs a hole for the eggs, then covers the eggs with sand and leaves them. Female turtles that live in rivers, lakes or ponds lay eggs near the waterside. When the babies hatch, they run to the water. Some female turtles stay close after the babies are born. Other turtles leave the babies to look after themselves.

A Loggerhead turtle

Shell for protection from enemies

Beak for biting and ripping food

Flippers for swimming

When baby turtles hatch, they run quickly down to the sea.

FOOD

A turtle usually eats animals it finds in the water. Freshwater turtles eat crayfish, fish, worms and voles. Sea turtles eat mostly jellyfish or sea plants. Turtles don't have teeth. They hold and rip food with their strong beaks.

Tyrannosaur

See also: Dinosaur, Fossil

The tyrannosaur was a powerful two-legged dinosaur. It had a massive head and jaws with rows of sharp teeth. It was as heavy as an elephant.

TYRANNOSAUR FACTS

COLOUR....not known
HEIGHT..... up to 5.6 m
LENGTH.... 12 m
WEIGHT.... about 7 tonnes

Lifestyle

The tyrannosaur was a hunter. It may have tracked herds of plant-eating dinosaurs. It could have caught its victims in its jaws.

The tyrannosaur twisted its head violently to rip flesh. Tyrannosaurs may also have eaten dead and rotting bodies.

Eyes that face forward to help in an attack

Long, heavy tail to balance the body

Hinged jaw so the mouth could open extra wide

Big claws to rip victims

Muscular thighs for running and attacking

A Tyrannosaurus Rex

FOOD

Tyrannosaurs ate other dinosaurs. They could grow sharp, new teeth as the old ones wore down.

Uganda

See also: Africa

Uganda is a country in east Africa. There is high, flat land in the middle. There are many lakes and mountains. The north-east is dry. The south-west is wet.

This is where the River Nile starts, at Jinja in Uganda.

Living and working

Most people in Uganda live in the countryside. Farmers grow cotton, coffee and tea to sell to other countries. Many fish are caught in the lakes and rivers. There are mines for metals including copper and gold.

A popular meal in Uganda is chicken or meat sauce poured on mashed plantains mixed with butter. Plantains are like bananas. Red beans and fish are cooked with tomatoes, onions and spices.

DID YOU KNOW?

Africa's largest lake, Lake Victoria, is partly in Uganda.

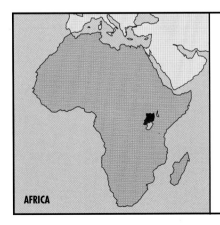

AFRICA

FACT FILE

PEOPLE........................ Ugandans
POPULATION................. 20.6 million
MAIN LANGUAGES .... English, Swahili
CAPITAL CITY.............. Kampala
MONEY .... Uganda shilling
HIGHEST MOUNTAIN .... Mount Margherita – 5119 m
LONGEST RIVER........... River Nile – 6670 km

Ukraine

See also: Europe

The Ukraine is a country in east Europe. It is mostly a large, flat area with rivers. In the west there are mountains, where it is cool. The Black Sea is to the south.

Living and working

Many people in the Ukraine live in towns and cities. They work in offices and factories. Farmers grow cereals and vegetables. They raise cattle and pigs. Mining is an important industry.

People bring different things to sell to this covered market in the capital city, Kiev.

The people enjoy eating food cooked with garlic, peppers and vinegar. A dish that is famous around the world is chicken kiev. This is chicken breast stuffed with garlic and butter. It is named after Kiev, the Ukraine's capital city.

DID YOU KNOW?

Sunflowers are one of the most important crops grown in the Ukraine.

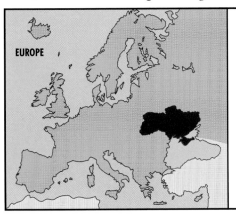

EUROPE

FACT FILE

PEOPLE	Ukrainians
POPULATION	51.5 million
MAIN LANGUAGE	Ukrainian
CAPITAL CITY	Kiev
MONEY	Hryvna
HIGHEST MOUNTAIN	Hoverla – 2058 m
LONGEST RIVER	River Dnieper – 2285 km

United Kingdom

See also: Europe

The United Kingdom (UK) is one country. It is made from four main parts: England, Scotland, Wales and Northern Ireland. The area sometimes called Great Britain is made up of England, Scotland and Wales.

Living and working

Most people live in the large towns or big cities. They work in offices, shops and factories. Farmers grow over half of the food eaten in the country. Fishing is important around the coasts. Fried fish and chips is one of the most popular meals in the UK.

The government of the UK meets in the Houses of Parliament, by the River Thames in London.

DID YOU KNOW?

The United Kingdom once ruled places in Africa, India, North America and Australia. These places are now separate countries. Most of the countries that used to be ruled from the UK are still members of a group called the Commonwealth.

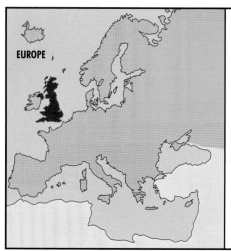

EUROPE

FACT FILE

PEOPLE...................... British, English, Northern Irish, Scottish, Welsh

POPULATION............... 58 million

CAPITAL CITY............. London

MAIN LANGUAGES....... English, Welsh, Gaelic (Irish and Scottish)

MONEY....................... Pound sterling

HIGHEST MOUNTAIN... Ben Nevis – 1343 m

LONGEST RIVER.......... River Severn – 338 km

United Nations

The United Nations is an organization that works to prevent wars and to help the world's people. Most of the countries in the world belong. The United Nations is sometimes called the UN.

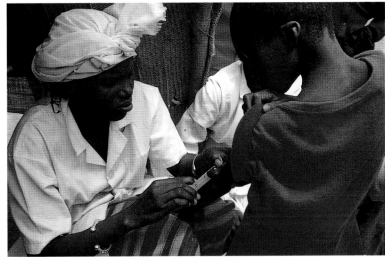

Many groups are part of the United Nations. Each of them has a special job. One group is the World Health Organization (WHO). This helps countries work together to fight diseases. Money from the WHO paid for these injections in Mali.

How the United Nations works

The headquarters of the United Nations is in New York City in the USA. It works in almost all the countries in the world. Once a year, people from the different countries meet at the UN's General Assembly, where they talk about things that are important to everyone in the world.

Peacekeeping

The most powerful countries belong to the UN Security Council. The Security Council borrows soldiers from member countries to use as a UN army, to try to stop people fighting. The UN has helped keep peace in the Middle East, New Guinea, Cyprus, Bosnia and Lebanon.

DID YOU KNOW?

UN soldiers wear blue hats and drive white trucks so that fighting armies can tell who they are.

This is the flag of the United Nations.

United States of America

See also: Native Americans, North America

The United States of America (USA) is a very large country in North America. There is a huge, flat area in the middle. The Rocky Mountains run from north to south in the west. Summers are hot. Winters in the north are very cold.

The Grand Canyon was made over millions of years by water wearing away soft rock and leaving the hard rock. Visitors can walk or travel by mule to the canyon bottom, but it is a long, tiring journey.

Living and working

Most Americans live in towns and cities. The people work in offices, shops and factories. The different climates in the USA are good for farmers to raise animals and grow all kinds of crops.

People have moved to the USA from all over the world. They brought the foods and traditions of their families. Americans also eat food that comes from the cultures of the Native Americans, like sweetcorn, squashes and turkey.

DID YOU KNOW?

There are 50 stars on the American flag. Each one stands for one of the 50 states. Florida, California and Texas are states.

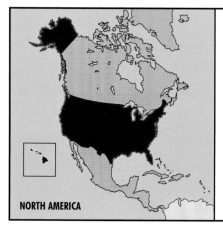

NORTH AMERICA

FACT FILE

PEOPLE......................Americans
POPULATION.............. 260.6 million
MAIN LANGUAGES...... English, Spanish
CAPITAL CITY........... Washington DC
LARGEST CITY...........New York City
MONEY.....................US dollar
HIGHEST MOUNTAIN ... Mount Denali (McKinley) – 6194 m
LONGEST RIVER......... Mississippi River – 3780 km

Valley

See also: Mountain, River

A valley is an area of low land, with higher land on both sides. There is usually a river or a stream in the valley bottom. The valley sides can be steep or very gentle. A deep valley with very steep sides is called a canyon, a gorge or a ravine.

How valleys are made

Valleys are made by the weather and by rivers. Rain and frost break up the ground into small pieces. The rivers carry the broken pieces away and cut a valley in the land.

Most mountain valleys are narrow and have steep sides. Rivers in mountain valleys flow over rapids and waterfalls. In the lowlands, valleys are usually much wider and slopes are more gentle.

A steep valley in mountains may only have a small stream in the bottom.

People often build roads, railways and canals along flat valley bottoms. It is easier to build along a valley than across mountains.

Valleys and people

The soil in a valley bottom is usually good for growing crops. It is also close to water if the crops need it. Valley sides that face the Sun become warm. This helps crops to grow faster.

DID YOU KNOW?

The Grand Canyon in the USA is a valley formed by the Colorado River. It is 1.6 km deep and about 16 km wide. It is wider in some places and narrower in others.

Venezuela

See also: South America

Venezuela is a country in South America. The weather in Venezuela is hot all year and there is a rainy season. There are rainforests and grasslands called *llanos*. Part of the Andes mountain range is in Venezuela.

Living and working

Most people live in the cities. A small number of people in Venezuela work on farms, growing maize, bananas, coffee and sugar. Cattle are raised to sell to other countries. Many people work in Venezuela's oilfields.

Venezuelans are descendants of native Indians, African slaves and people from Spain. They celebrate the main Christian festivals at Easter, Christmas and on local saints' days.

The capital of Venezuela, Caracas, is a large, modern city. The Andes Mountains tower above the city.

DID YOU KNOW?

Columbus Day is an important festival in Venezuela. It reminds people that Christopher Columbus landed in Venezuela in 1498.

SOUTH
AMERICA

FACT FILE

PEOPLE........................ Venezuelans
POPULATION .... 21.4 million
MAIN LANGUAGE .... Spanish
CAPITAL CITY .... Caracas
MONEY........................ Bolívar
HIGHEST MOUNTAIN.... Merida – 5007 m
LONGEST RIVER .... River Orinoco – 2500 km

Vertebrate

See also: Invertebrate, Skeleton

Vertebrates are animals that have skeletons with backbones inside their bodies. All mammals, including human beings, are vertebrates. Having a backbone helps an animal to move quickly and change direction easily. Animals as different as dogs, whales and seagulls are all vertebrates.

Dinosaurs were vertebrates. Some, like this triceratops, had huge skeletons.

The seven kinds of vertebrates

There are seven different kinds of animals that are vertebrates. One kind of fish have backbones but no other skeleton. Sharks and similar fish have skeletons, including a backbone, but it is made of a strong material called cartilage, not bones. Other fish, all amphibians, reptiles, birds and mammals are vertebrates with skeletons and backbones made from bone.

Most bony vertebrates have skulls and ribs. A lot of vertebrates have two or four limbs, which may be two arms and two legs, or four legs.

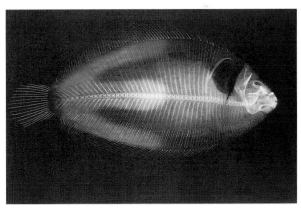

You can see from this X-ray of a sole fish that it is a vertebrate.

DID YOU KNOW?

Another word for the backbone is the spine.

Vietnam

See also: Asia

Vietnam is a country in south-east Asia. The weather is mostly hot. There is a dry season and a wet season. There are tropical rainforests over one-third of the country. Tigers, monkeys and other animals live in the forests.

The style of the buildings in Ho Chi Minh City is French. France ruled Vietnam from the 1850s to the 1950s.

Living and working

Most of the people in Vietnam work on farms. Farmers grow rice in small fields on flat land. People also catch fish to eat. Some people work in factories making paper, cloth, chemicals and steel.

Vietnam became one country in 1975 after a long war. Many homes, roads, farms and factories were destroyed during the war.

DID YOU KNOW?

There is a huge New Year festival in Vietnam. It is called the Tet Festival and it is held at the time of the first new moon in the new year.

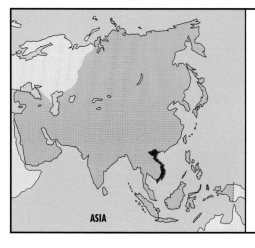

ASIA

FACT FILE

PEOPLE	Vietnamese
POPULATION	73.1 million
MAIN LANGUAGE	Vietnamese
CAPITAL CITY	Hanoi
LARGEST CITY	Ho Chi Minh City
MONEY	Dong
HIGHEST MOUNTAIN	Fan Si Pan – 3143 m
LONGEST RIVER	Mekong River – 4500 km

Vikings

See also: Denmark, Norway, Sweden

Vikings were lots of different groups of people from Norway, Sweden and Denmark. They spread out across Europe, raiding settlements and taking over land as they went.

What were the Vikings like?

Vikings were warriors and farmers. They lived in small groups. They had a few towns and trading ports where Vikings from different groups met and traded with each other. Vikings believed in many gods and goddesses who controlled the world.

KEY DATES

780 AD......Vikings first raid Europe

800 AD......Vikings settle in France and the Netherlands

841 AD......First Viking settlements built in western Europe and in Dublin, Ireland

860s AD....Vikings trade with Russia and raid Italy and North Africa

986 AD.....The first Viking sighting of North America (they landed some years later)

1070 AD
onwards... The Vikings stop taking land and slowly take on the ways and beliefs of the countries they settle in

What are the Vikings famous for?

The Vikings are famous for their beautiful, wooden longships. They may even have crossed the Atlantic Ocean in them and discovered North America long before Christopher Columbus did. They are also famous for their sagas. These are stories about the past and the lives of the gods.

The Vikings made many beautiful things from bronze. This ornament is supposed to be the god, Odin.

This Viking longship was built in about 850 AD.

Virus

See also: Bacteria

A virus is a very small living thing that is found in the soil, the air, or in a plant or animal. A virus can cause a disease in a person or animal. Some viruses can stay in the air for a long time, doing nothing, until a person or animal breathes it in. The virus can then start making new viruses. A virus is too small to see except with a very powerful microscope.

VIRUS FACTS

NUMBER OF KINDS	many
COLOUR	any
SIZE	very small
LIFE SPAN	hundreds of years
ENEMIES	some medicines

Diseases

Diseases caused by viruses include chicken pox, measles, rabies, flu and the common cold. A person or animal that gets a virus makes special cells called antibodies to try to kill the virus. This can make them better. Doctors use weak or dead viruses to make medicines to keep people from getting those viruses. This protection is called immunization.

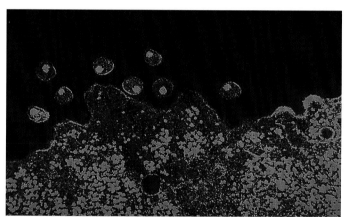

HIV is a virus which causes the disease known as AIDS. It is spread by infected body fluids.

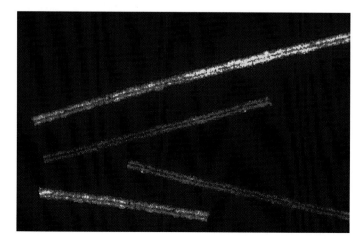

FOOD

A virus does not eat. It steals bits of living cells and uses them to make more viruses the same as itself.

This is the herpes virus. It can cause coldsores.

Volcano

See also: Mountain

A volcano is a mountain with a hole down the middle. It is usually cone-shaped. Hot, melted rock from deep under the Earth's surface can push up through the hole. Then ashes, burning gases and hot rock, called magma, burst out through the top. When this happens, the volcano is erupting. The hot rock that runs down the sides of the mountain is called lava.

How a volcano is made

When the hot lava flows down the sides of the volcano it cools down and goes hard. Every time the volcano erupts, more layers of lava make the volcano grow bigger. There are three types of volcano.

- An active volcano is one that still erupts. There are 535 active volcanoes on the Earth.
- A dormant volcano has not erupted for hundreds of years, but it may erupt again.
- An extinct volcano will never erupt again.

DID YOU KNOW?

The biggest volcano that people know about is on the planet Mars. It is about 25 km high and about 100 km across.

Molten lava is streaming down from this volcano in Hawaii.

People and volcanoes

It can be very dangerous to live near an active volcano. Volcanoes can also be useful. The soil near a volcano can be very good for farming. There is often hot water in the ground where there are volcanoes. This is used for bathing and to heat people's homes.

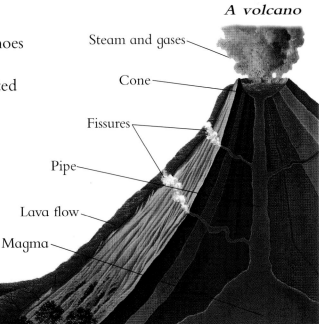

A volcano

Steam and gases

Cone

Fissures

Pipe

Lava flow

Magma

Vulture

See also: Bird

A vulture is a large bird which eats dead or dying animals. Different kinds of vultures live all over the world. Vultures are good fliers, and they soar above the ground looking for dead or dying animals.

Vulture families

Some vultures build a nest in a cave or tree. Others just lay their eggs inside a dead tree. Vultures lay one or two eggs.

The parents share the work of looking after the chicks. After the babies have left the nest, they will often stay with their parents for one or two years.

VULTURE FACTS

NUMBER OF KINDS	20
COLOUR	black, white or grey
LENGTH	up to 1.1 m
WEIGHT	up to 13 kg
STATUS	common
LIFE SPAN	about 20 years
ENEMIES	none

Bald neck and head to keep clean while eating

Sharp beak for pecking at food

Good eyes to spot food from the sky

Strong claws for tearing food

Powerful wings for soaring in the air

A Ruppell's vulture

FOOD

Vultures eat animals that have died or have been killed by other animals. They also eat food they find at rubbish dumps. Sometimes they eat eggs and insects. Most vultures have no feathers on their necks and feet, so that they can reach deep into dead animals without getting their feathers dirty.

This young white-backed vulture is resting in its nest.

Wales

See also: Europe, United Kingdom

Wales is one of the four main parts of the United Kingdom. Mountains cover most of Wales. There is some lowland in the south. There are many sandy beaches and bays along the coast. The weather in Wales is often wet with clouds over the mountains.

Living and working

Much of the mountain land in Wales is used to raise sheep. Tourists visit the mountains to go climbing, camping and to enjoy the views. There are old mining villages in the south, and there are factories which make iron and steel. Most people now work in new factories and offices in the cities. Cardiff and Swansea are the biggest cities. Many people speak the Welsh language. Rugby is a favourite Welsh sport.

The Welsh national costume is still worn for traditional events such as the National Eisteddfodd, the festival of Welsh singing and poetry.

DID YOU KNOW?

Wales is famous for its poets and its male-voice choirs.

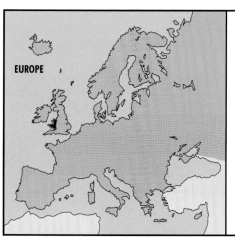

EUROPE

FACT FILE

PEOPLE........................ Welsh
POPULATION............... 2.9 million
MAIN LANGUAGES....... English and Welsh
CAPITAL CITY............. Cardiff
MONEY....................... Pound sterling
HIGHEST MOUNTAIN... Snowdon – 1085 m
LONGEST RIVER.......... River Dee – 145 km

Wasp

See also: Bee, Insect

A wasp is an insect that can sting. There are many kinds of wasps which live all around the world. The wasp's black and yellow colours warn birds, lizards and frogs not to eat them. The sting of a wasp is poisonous, although it usually won't kill a human being.

Wasp families

The most important female wasp is called the queen. The queen wasp mates with males in the autumn. She finds a place to hibernate until the spring. In the spring, the queen wakes up and builds a nest, where she lays her eggs. The nest is made of chewed wood or paper.

The eggs become larvae, and the first ones to hatch look after the others. Some larvae become males, most become female workers that never breed and a few become new queens.

FOOD

A wasp eats small insects, caterpillars and fruit.

WASP FACTS

NUMBER OF KINDS	25,000
COLOUR	black and yellow
LENGTH	up to 18 mm
STATUS	common
LIFE SPAN	about 4 weeks (queens 10 months)
ENEMIES	birds, people

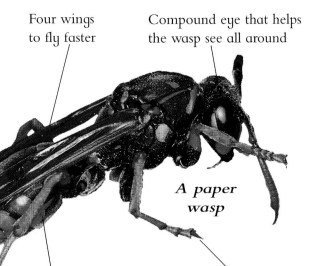

Four wings to fly faster

Compound eye that helps the wasp see all around

A paper wasp

Bright yellow and black colours to frighten off enemies

Clawed legs grip things

The sting can be used many times

These hornet wasps are in their nest.

Water

See also: Water cycle

Water is the most common liquid in the world. It covers more than half of the Earth. Fresh, clean, unsalty water is very precious. Without water to drink, human beings and most other animals could live only a few days.

WATER FACTS

FORMS	solid ice, liquid water, gassy steam
FREEZING TEMPERATURE	0°C
BOILING TEMPERATURE	100°C
CHEMICAL FORMULA	H_2O. This means it is made up of hydrogen and oxygen

Water and life on Earth

All plants and animals need water to keep alive. The human body is four-fifths (80%) water. People and many living things need fresh water. There is water in streams, rivers and lakes. This is called fresh water because it is not salty. Fresh water is also found under the ground. Water is found in the oceans and seas all over the world. This water is salty and is not good for people to drink or cook with. Some animals, fish and plants live in and near salty water.

People and water

People use water every day to drink, to cook and to wash. Water in many countries is brought into houses in pipes. It comes from water treatment works where it is cleaned. People also use the power of moving water to make electricity. People can also have fun in water, for example when they swim.

Water is treated in a water-treatment works, before it is sent to people's homes.

Fresh water for people is often stored in huge man-made lakes, called reservoirs. Sometimes they are made by building a dam across a river.

Water cycle

See also: Water

The water cycle is the way that the Earth is supplied with fresh water. Water from the sea makes rain. Rain falls and runs into the ground, then into rivers and back to the seas. Energy from the Sun keeps the water cycle running.

How the water cycle works

As the Sun shines onto seas and lakes, water evaporates to form water vapour. As the water vapour rises, it cools. As it cools, it forms tiny drops of water, which make up clouds. Rain then falls from the clouds. The fresh rainwater seeps into the soil. Plants suck up some of the water. The rest collects together and runs into rivers and streams. The rivers eventually flow back into the sea.

Saving water

If people use too much water the natural water cycle can be damaged. Taking too much water from a river can make it dry up. In some countries the rainy season doesn't come. Then plants don't grow and animals and people suffer.

The water cycle.

Waterway

See also: Barge, Ship, Transport

A waterway is a man-made river. Waterways are used by boats and ships, and are sometimes called canals.

The first waterways

The Chinese built the first waterways over 2000 years ago. They discovered that it was easier to carry heavy loads on water than on land. Waterways were built to connect rivers. Later, special steps with gates, called locks, were used. They allow waterways to go up and down hills.

People and waterways

Many small waterways are now used just for holiday boats. It is quicker to travel by train or car than on the water. Big waterways are still important for ships.

One important waterway is called the Panama Canal. It joins the Atlantic Ocean and the Pacific Ocean between North and South America. Ships use the canal so that they don't have to go round the south of South America to get from one ocean to the other.

Barges towed by horses were used on canals. Some canals still have a walkway next to them, called the tow path. Most canal barges are now used as houseboats or for holidays.

IMPORTANT WORLD WATERWAYS

SUEZ CANAL	1869
CORINTH CANAL	1893
MANCHESTER SHIP CANAL	1894
PANAMA CANAL	1914
ST LAWRENCE SEAWAY	1959
VOLGA–BALTIC WATERWAY	1964

The Corinth Canal in Greece is used by large ships to save time.

Weather

See also: Climate

Weather is the temperature, the wind, how many clouds there are, whether it is sunny, cloudy, dry or rainy outside. The weather in a place can depend on the time of year and where the place is in the world.

What causes different types of weather?

The energy the Sun sends to the Earth make all the types of weather. When air near to the ground gets warm, it rises. New air rushes in to take its place. This makes wind. As the warm air goes higher, it cools down. This makes clouds and rain. If the raindrops freeze, they make hailstones. Electricity can build up in big clouds. This makes lightning and thunder. In very cold clouds, tiny ice crystals form. These fall as snowflakes.

What will the weather be like?

People called meteorologists study the weather. They use satellite pictures, balloons, computers and information from weather stations to work out what they think will happen. This is called weather forecasting.

Bad weather, such as this thunderstorm in Australia, can cause damage and cut off electricity supplies.

DID YOU KNOW?

Hurricanes and tornadoes are storms with very strong winds. Winds reaching 320 kph can destroy trees, houses and cars.

Whale

See also: Dolphin, Mammal

A whale is a large mammal which lives in the sea. There are many different kinds of whale living in all the world's oceans and seas. Many whales migrate from cold to warmer water during the year.

Whale families

Most female whales breed only once every two to three years. Adult whales meet up in an area of warm sea, where they mate.

Female whales come back to this place to have their calves. Each female has one calf, which she feeds with her milk. A calf may stay with its mother for several years.

WHALE FACTS

NUMBER OF KINDS	83
COLOUR	blue, grey, white
LENGTH	up to 26 m
WEIGHT	up to 130 tonnes
STATUS	some endangered
LIFE SPAN	about 80 years
ENEMIES	People used to hunt whales for oil. Some people still hunt whales for meat and for scientific purposes.

This humpback whale is feeding.

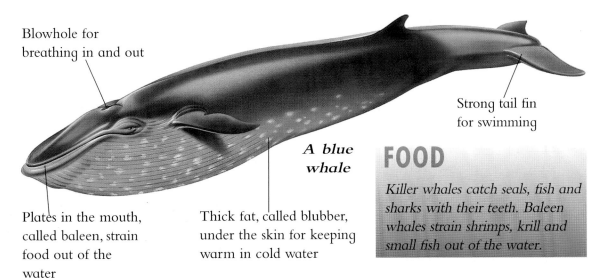

Blowhole for breathing in and out

Strong tail fin for swimming

A blue whale

Plates in the mouth, called baleen, strain food out of the water

Thick fat, called blubber, under the skin for keeping warm in cold water

FOOD

Killer whales catch seals, fish and sharks with their teeth. Baleen whales strain shrimps, krill and small fish out of the water.

Wind instruments

See also: Music, Musical instrument

Wind instruments are played by blowing air into them to make sounds. In most wind instruments, the air is blown from the player's mouth.

The first wind instruments
Ancient peoples made wind instruments from hollow wood and animal horns. Aboriginal Australians play an instrument called a *didgeridoo,* which is a wind instrument made from a hollow piece of wood. A special sheep's horn, called a *shofar,* is blown at the Jewish festivals of Rosh Hashanah and Yom Kippur.

Woodwind and brass instruments
The two main kinds of wind instrument used in music today are woodwinds and brass instruments. Woodwinds include clarinets, flutes, oboes, *cor anglais,* bassoons and saxophones. Brass instruments include trumpets, trombones, French horns and tubas.

The bagpipes are played in several countries. This Scottish piper is dressed in traditional Scottish highland dress.

Clarinet

French horn

The French horn is a brass instrument. The clarinet is a woodwind instrument.

DID YOU KNOW?

The bagpipes are a wind instrument. The air is blown into a bag and then pushed out through pipes. One or more of the pipes can be used to play a tune. There can be others which make low background sounds. The bagpipes are traditional instruments in many countries, including Scotland and Ireland.

Wolf

See also: Dog, Mammal

A wolf is a kind of wild dog. It is a mammal and lives in Russia, Canada, the United States and in parts of Europe.

Wolf families

A wolf lives in a group called a pack. Many adult wolves in the pack do not have babies. They help other pack members to bring up young wolves by hunting for food for them. A female wolf that is expecting babies digs out an underground den. She has between four and seven cubs that she feeds on milk for about two months. When the cubs are old enough to eat meat, all the adults in the pack bring home meat for them.

WOLF FACTS

NUMBER OF KINDS	2
COLOUR	grey, white, brown
HEIGHT	up to 81 cm
LENGTH	up to 1.6 m
WEIGHT	up to 80 kg
STATUS	common
LIFE SPAN	about 16 years
ENEMIES	people

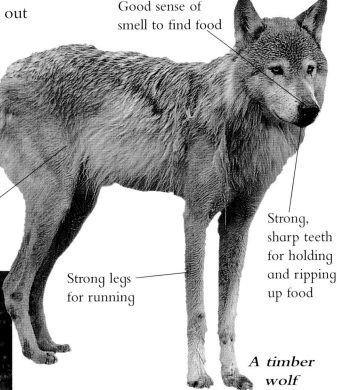

Good sense of smell to find food

Thick fur for keeping warm in cold weather

Strong, sharp teeth for holding and ripping up food

Strong legs for running

A timber wolf

This grey wolf and her cub are white in the winter so that they can hide against the snow.

FOOD

A wolf eats deer, moose, wild sheep, dead animals and berries. It will also kill and eat farm animals. The pack will work together to surround and kill a large animal.

Wolverine

See also: Mammal

A wolverine is an endangered mammal. It lives in northern areas of the world, especially in North America.

Wolverine families

The wolverine lives on its own during most of the year, and has a big territory. In the summer wolverines meet and the males and females mate. Each adult female has babies only once every two or three years.

She digs a den in the ground or in the snow. Here up to four babies, called kittens, are born. The mother looks after them, feeding them on milk or on food she has buried earlier. Female kittens stay with their mother for two years, but males leave home after one year to live on their own.

FOOD

A wolverine will eat almost any meat it finds. In the summer it eats small mammals, birds and birds' eggs. In the winter it can kill and eat large animals such as reindeer, which are much bigger than itself. It will also steal dead animals from bears.

WOLVERINE FACTS

NUMBER OF KINDS	2
COLOUR	mixed browns and white
LENGTH	up to 105 cm
WEIGHT	up to 32 kg
STATUS	rare
LIFE SPAN	up to 13 years
ENEMIES	People hunt wolverines for their fur.

A wolverine

Thick fur for keeping out the cold

Big feet to walk on snow without sinking in

Five sharp claws for fighting and digging

Strong teeth for crushing bones

Young kits stay near their den.

Wood

See also: Forest, Rainforest, Tree

Wood is an important natural material that comes from trees. Each tree has its own type of wood with special uses. People have used wood for at least a million years.

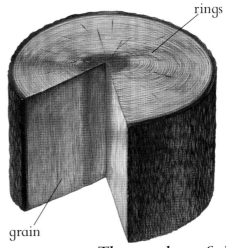

The number of rings shows how old the tree is.

How wood is formed

Wood is the solid part inside the trunks of trees and shrubs. As a tree grows, its trunk gets thicker. When a tree trunk is cut across, rings can be seen in the wood. New wood is made just under the bark of a tree. Each ring is one year's growth. The number of rings in its trunk can give the age of the tree. When the trunk is cut into timber the rings make the grain of the wood.

Kinds of wood

Hardwoods come from broad-leaved trees that grow quite slowly, such as oak and mahogany. Many hardwoods are strong. Softwoods come from conifers such as fir and pine trees that grow very quickly. The wood is usually lighter and weaker than hardwoods.

Using wood

People use wood in may ways. In some places wood is burned as a fuel for heating and cooking. In lots of places wood is used for building houses. Furniture is made from wood. Paper is made from wood pulp. Many musical instruments, toys and household ornaments are made from wood.

Wood is used in furniture factories, like this, to make table tops and other things.

DID YOU KNOW?

It is not always necessary to cut a tree down to find out how old it is. Tree specialists can bore into the trunk and take a small section out of the tree, to count the rings. Some trees are over 3000 years old.

Woodlouse

See also: Crustacean, Invertebrate

A woodlouse is a crustacean, like crabs and lobsters. It is an invertebrate. It lives on dry land, although it likes damp places. There are many species of woodlouse living in most areas of the world.

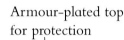

WOODLOUSE FACTS

NUMBER OF KINDS	many
COLOUR	brown when young, then grey
LENGTH	about 15mm
STATUS	common
LIFE SPAN	a few months
ENEMIES	birds, frogs, small mammals

Woodlouse families

The woodlouse lives under logs, leaves and stones, or in damp parts of houses. It comes out only at night when the air is damp. The woodlouse does not build a nest. The woodlouse has babies, which are very like the adults only smaller.

Armour-plated top for protection

Feelers to help find things

A woodlouse

FOOD

A woodlouse eats decaying plants, including wood and fungi. It finds its food in old logs in the forest, or in houses where wood is beginning to rot.

These woodlice are feeding on rotten, damp wood.

Woodpecker

See also: Bird

A woodpecker is a bird with a special beak and head. Woodpeckers can drill holes in trees to make nests and to look for food. Woodpeckers live in trees all over the world.

Woodpecker families

Most woodpeckers live on their own in the winter. In the spring, they find a mate by singing and making a noise drumming on trees with their beaks. Each pair makes a new hole in a tree or uses an old one. When the nest hole is ready, the female woodpecker lays five to seven eggs.

The red-shafted flicker is a kind of woodpecker. The male is feeding his hungry chicks.

WOODPECKER FACTS

NUMBER OF KINDS	210
COLOUR	mainly black, black and white, green or brown
LENGTH	up to 50 cm
WEIGHT	up to 700 g
STATUS	common
LIFE SPAN	about 7 years
ENEMIES	Woodpeckers need old trees, which people sometimes clear away.

Long, sticky tongue to capture ants and other insects

Feathers over the nostrils keep out wood dust

Long, strong, beak for making holes

Very thick skin to protect from ant bites

Long, clawed feet for climbing tree trunks

A woodpecker and its chick

FOOD

A woodpecker eats ants and other insects. It also eats fruit and seeds. It drinks from water trapped in old trees.

World War I

See also: World War II

World War I began in 1914. It ended in 1918. It was called a world war because powerful countries from many parts of the world fought in it.

Why was there a war?

The most powerful countries in Europe tried to build up land and power in other places. They did not trust each other. They began to take sides. Germany, Austria and Turkey were on one side. Britain, France, Italy and Russia were on the other. They began to plan what to do if there was a war. When an Austrian prince was killed in Serbia, Austria blamed Serbia. Russia supported Serbia, Germany supported Austria, and Britain and France supported Russia. The war began.

What happened in the war?

Both sides expected the war would be over by Christmas 1914. It lasted four years. Millions of people were killed. As the war went on, other countries joined in, including the USA. In November 1918 Germany gave in.

All the countries that fought signed an agreement called the Treaty of Versailles. This took away lots of German land. Germany also had to pay money to other countries and was only allowed to have a small army.

KEY DATES

28 JUNE 1914	Austrian prince, Franz Ferdinand is killed
28 JULY 1914	Austria goes to war with Serbia
30 JULY 1914	Russia goes to war with Austria
1 AND 3 AUGUST 1914	Germany enters war against Russia, then France
4 AUGUST 1914	Britain joins the war
6 APRIL 1917	USA joins the war
11 NOVEMBER 1918	The war ends

Soldiers fighting in France fought and lived in ditches, called trenches, like these.

World War II

See also: World War I

World War II began in 1939. It ended in 1945. It was called a world war because powerful and important countries from many parts of the world fought in it.

Why was there a war?

Germany was angry about how it was treated after World War I. From 1933 on, Adolf Hitler and the Nazis took power in Germany. They built up the German army, which took back the land taken from Germany after World War I. In 1938, Germany invaded Czechoslovakia. The rest of Europe hoped it would stop there. But in 1939 Germany invaded Poland. The war had started.

What happened in the war?

At first, Germany and Italy were at war against the Allies – Britain and France. When Germany invaded Russia in June 1941, Russia joined the Allies. In 1941, Japan attacked a United States navy base. This pulled the USA into the war, on the side of the Allies.

A new weapon, the atomic bomb, was invented during the war. When Germany gave in, but Japan did not, the US dropped atomic bombs on two cities in Japan. The cities were completely destroyed. Japan gave in and the war was over.

KEY DATES

1 SEPTEMBER 1939...Germany invades Poland. UK declares war on Germany

APRIL–MAY 1940.....Germany invades Norway, Denmark, then Belgium, the Netherlands and France

JUNE 1941..............Germany invades Russia

7 DECEMBER 1941...Japan and USA join the war

MAY 1945...............Germany gives in. The war in Europe ends

AUGUST 1945..........Atomic bombs dropped on Japan

2 SEPTEMBER 1945...Japan gives in. The war ends

London, like many other cities, was heavily bombed during World War II.

Worm

See also: Invertebrate

A worm is an animal with a long, soft body. Some worms, such as roundworms or flatworms, are very simple creatures. Others, such as earthworms and leeches, have bodies divided into several segments.

Worm families

Most kinds of worm don't have males and females. Almost all worms lay eggs. They hatch after a few weeks. They can look after themselves from the time they are born. Most worms make a burrow to live in.

WORM FACTS

NUMBER OF KINDS	many thousands
COLOUR	all
LENGTH	up to 3 m (giant Australian worm)
STATUS	common
LIFE SPAN	about 2 years
ENEMIES	birds, foxes, badgers

No eyes are needed underground

This is called the saddle. Eggs are laid from here

Body segments for wriggling

An earthworm

FOOD

Different kinds of worm eat different things. Earthworms and lugworms eat leaves or pieces of seaweed which they find over or under the soil or sand.

This earthworm is pulling a big leaf to eat into the ground.

Yugoslavia

See also: Europe

Yugoslavia is a country in east Europe. In the north there is lowland with rivers. There are mountains and hills in the centre and south. Summers are warm. Winters are cold. The coast is hotter.

Many Yugoslavians work in the shops and offices of the capital city, Belgrade.

Living and working

About half the people in Yugoslavia live in the countryside. Farmers grow grains, sugar beet, potatoes, cotton and grapes. They also raise pigs, sheep and cattle. There is mining for oil, gas, coal, lead, copper and zinc. There are factories making textiles and machinery.

Yugoslavia used to be a bigger country, with six parts. Since 1992 it has been made up of just the republics of Serbia and Montenegro. Fighting between the old parts of Yugoslavia made life hard.

DID YOU KNOW?

Serbian food mixes interesting things together. One popular dish contains fried peppers, bacon, prunes, tomatoes and spices.

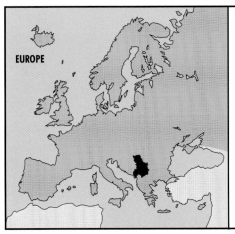

EUROPE

FACT FILE

PEOPLE...................... Yugoslavians, Serbians, Montenegrins

POPULATION.............. 10.6 million

MAIN LANGUAGE......... Serbian

CAPITAL CITY............. Belgrade

MONEY...................... New dinar

HIGHEST MOUNTAIN... Durmitor – 2522 m

LONGEST RIVER.......... River Danube – 2850 km

Zambia

See also: Africa

Zambia is a country in Africa. Most of the country is high, flat land. There is one hot, wet season and a warm, dry season. Forests cover one-third of the country. The rest is grassland with scattered trees. There are herds of giraffes, elephants and rhinoceroses. Crocodiles and hippos live in the rivers.

The Victoria Falls on the River Zambezi is the largest waterfall in Africa.

Living and working

About one-third of the people in Zambia work on farms. Maize is the main crop. There is mining for copper in an area called 'the Copper Belt'.

There are many different groups of people in Zambia. They speak about 70 different types of the Bantu language and have their own local customs.

DID YOU KNOW?

The famous explorer David Livingstone was the first European to see the Victoria Falls.

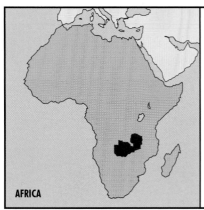

AFRICA

FACT FILE

PEOPLE	Zambians
POPULATION	9.2 million
MAIN LANGUAGES	English, Bantu languages
CAPITAL CITY	Lusaka
MONEY	Kwacha
HIGHEST MOUNTAIN	Nyika plateau – 2164 m
LONGEST RIVER	Zambezi – 3540 km

Zebra

See also: Horse, Mammal

A zebra is a black and white mammal which lives in southern and eastern Africa. It is a member of the horse family.

Zebra families

A male zebra is called a stallion. A female zebra is called a mare. Zebras live in groups called herds. In a herd there is one stallion and five or six mares and their foals. The stallion walks at the back of the herd to watch out enemies.

The mares have one foal each in the spring. One hour after it is born, the foal is ready to walk with the herd. The young stay with the herd for about two years. Then young stallions join other males until they are old enough to have a herd of their own.

ZEBRA FACTS

NUMBER OF KINDS	3
COLOUR	black and white
HEIGHT	1.8 m
LENGTH	up to 2.6 m
WEIGHT	372 kg
STATUS	common
LIFE SPAN	up to 28 years
ENEMIES	lions, cheetahs, leopards

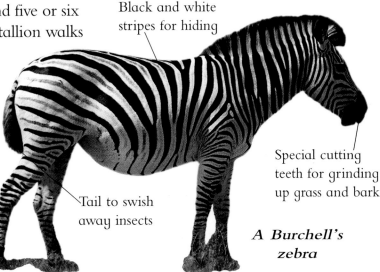

Black and white stripes for hiding

Special cutting teeth for grinding up grass and bark

Tail to swish away insects

A Burchell's zebra

FOOD

A zebra eats grass. When a zebra cannot find enough grass, it eats bark, buds and fruit. A zebra can survive for three days without drinking water.

This female zebra and her foal live in a wildlife reserve in Kenya.

Zimbabwe

See also: Africa

Zimbabwe is a country in southern Africa. There is high, flat land with mountains to the east. The land is low in the north and south. Summers are hot and wet. Winters are warm.

Zimbabwe's villages often have traditional round houses.

Living and working

Most people in Zimbabwe live in the countryside. Maize is the main crop grown for food. The farmers also grow tobacco, cotton and sugar beet to sell to other countries. Mining is very important.

Farmers also raise a lot of cattle and goats. A favourite meat dish is grilled beef with peppers, tamarinds and bay leaves. A tamarind is a kind of large seed pod. This dish is served with soft balls of ground maize. Women in Zimbabwe make clothes and jewellery using fine beadwork. Many houses are decorated with colourful geometric designs.

DID YOU KNOW?

The name of Zimbabwe means 'stone houses'. Great Zimbabwe was a huge stone city built nearly 1000 years ago by the Shona people.

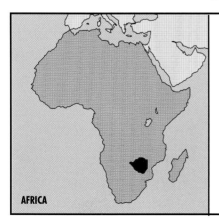

AFRICA

FACT FILE

PEOPLE	Zimbabweans
POPULATION	11 million
MAIN LANGUAGES	English, Shona, Ndebele
CAPITAL CITY	Harare
MONEY	Zimbabwe dollar
HIGHEST MOUNTAIN	Inyangani – 2592 m
LONGEST RIVER	River Zambezi – 3540 km